Clifton Park - Halfmoon Public Library

W9-BAK-160

Structural Wonders

Beijing National Stadium

Sheelagh Matthews

Clifton Park - Halfmoon Public Library
475 Moe Road
Clifton Park, New York 12065

W

Published by Weigl Publishers Inc.
350 5th Avenue, Suite 3304, PMB 6G
New York, NY 10118-0069

Website: www.weigl.com

Copyright ©2010 WEIGL PUBLISHERS INC.
All rights reserved. No part of this publication may be reproduced, stored
in a retrieval system, or transmitted in any form or by any means, electronic,
mechanical, photocopying, recording, or otherwise, without the prior written
permission of Weigl Publishers Inc.

Library of Congress Cataloging-in-Publication Data

Matthews, Sheelagh.
 Beijing National Stadium / Sheelagh Matthews.
     p. cm. -- (Structural wonders)
 Includes index.
 ISBN 978-1-60596-140-8 (hard cover : alk. paper) --
 ISBN 978-1-60596-141-5 (soft cover : alk. paper)
 1. Beijing guo jia ti yu chang (Beijing, China)--Juvenile literature.
 2. Beijing (China)--Buildings, structures, etc.--Juvenile literature. I. Title.
 NA6862.C62B455 2009
 725'.8270951156--dc22
                                        2009008364

Printed in China
1 2 3 4 5 6 7 8 9 0 13 12 11 10 09

7215

Photograph Credits
Every reasonable effort has been made to trace ownership and to obtain
permission to reprint copyright material. The publishers would be pleased
to have any errors or omissions brought to their attention so that they may
be corrected in subsequent printings.

Weigl acknowledges Getty Images as its primary image supplier for this title.

All of the internet URLs given in the book were valid at the time of publication.
However, due to the dynamic nature of the Internet, some addresses may have
changed, or sites may have ceased to exist since publication. While the author
and publisher regret any inconvenience this may cause readers, no responsibility
for any such changes can be accepted by either the author or the publisher.

Project Coordinators: Heather C. Hudak, Heather Kissock
Design: Terry Paulhus

Contents

5 What is the Beijing National Stadium?

6 Building History

8 Big Ideas

10 Profile

12 The Science Behind the Building

14 Science and Technology

16 Computer-Aided Design

19 Measuring the Beijing National Stadium

20 Environmental Viewpoint

22 Construction Careers

24 Notable Structures

26 Structural Icons Around the World

28 Quiz

29 The Nest Test

30 Further Research

31 Glossary

32 Index

What is the Beijing National Stadium?

The Beijing National Stadium is a symbol of the long-held dream of the Chinese people to host the Olympics. An exciting and attention-getting structure, the National Stadium was a centerpiece of the Beijing 2008 Summer Olympic Games. This structure has been nicknamed the "Bird's Nest" due to its twig-like **latticework** of steel **girders**.

This "bird's nest" design is rooted in Chinese art and culture. The building's designers used Chinese **ceramics** as their inspiration. However, it was important to China that the building portray more than the past. They also wanted it to show the world how modern China had become as a country. The design was to be bold and innovative. In combining elements of China's past and present, the National Stadium has become a culture-defining landmark for the country.

Almost one billion people marveled at this structure's design as they watched the Olympic Opening Ceremonies. Dramatic lighting and special effects transformed the stadium into a giant stage. Brilliant fireworks skyrocketed from its open roof as thousands of drummers, dancers, and athletes entertained below.

The National Stadium was built to host the Olympic track and field events, soccer, and athletics. However, the building was also made to be flexible for other uses. Today, it is used for large-scale sporting competitions, as well as cultural and entertainment events. Plans are also underway to connect a shopping mall and hotel to the structure.

Quick Bites

- The Olympic Games are the world's most important athletic games. Top athletes from all over the world compete in them. The games are held every four years.
- In 2008, the National Stadium hosted the 13th Paralympic Games, an international sports competition for physically challenged athletes. As a result, more spaces for wheelchairs were incorporated into the structure's design.

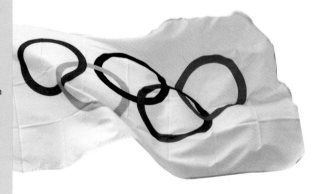

Building History

Beijing was awarded the 2008 Olympic Games in 2001. Shortly after, designers from all around the world were invited to submit their proposals to build an **iconic** stadium for the Beijing Olympics. After they were reviewed by experts, the entries were whittled down to 13. These 13 entries were then displayed to the public. Both experts and the public chose the same design as the winner. That entry was the "Bird's Nest."

The **groundbreaking ceremonies** for the National Stadium took place on December 24, 2003. Then, the real work began. **Architects**, engineers, and construction crews faced a deadline that could not be moved—the Olympics. There were only four years to get this enormous job done. Construction of this national icon had to meet tight schedules.

The National Stadium cost $423 million to build.

Within a few months of starting, however, the project began running into financial problems. In 2004, construction was stopped while the team came up with cost-saving measures. One of these changes was the removal of the **retractable** roof the building was supposed to have. Instead of the roof, the rooftop opening was enlarged. These change meant 22.3 percent less steel and 13 percent less **membrane** would be needed for the structure, saving on both money and materials.

The translucent membrane on the roof keeps out rain and lets sunlight through for natural lighting.

TIMELINE OF CONSTRUCTION

2002: Proposals are requested from around the world for plans to construct the National Stadium.

April 2003: The "Bird's Nest" is announced as the winning design.

December 24, 2003: Groundbreaking ceremonies for the National Stadium begin the official countdown to the 2008 Olympics.

August 2004: Construction is stopped due to cost overruns. The retractable roof design is cancelled to help save costs.

2005: Construction resumes.

2006: The concrete parts of the stadium are completed. The stadium's steel structure is welded together.

2007: *Time Magazine* names the National Stadium among "The 10 Best (New and Upcoming) Architectural Wonders." The "Bird's Nest" official website is launched.

2008: The 80,000 permanent seats are installed in January. Doors open to the public in April. The Olympic Summer Games are held from August 8 to 24.

The Olympic Countdown Clock, a giant digital timepiece in Tian'anmen Square, provided a countdown to the start of the Olympic Games.

While these changes were significant, they did not alter the concept of the "nest" structure. In fact, a larger rooftop opening made the structure more nest-like.

Seemingly random steel blends the supporting steel columns into the rest of the stadium. This "random additional steel" creates the look of the "Bird's Nest."

Construction resumed on the stadium at the beginning of 2005. This time, the work moved forward as planned. The stadium was opened to the public on April 18, 2008, with all work completed the next month—just three months before the Olympics began. Despite the structure's many design and construction challenges, an Olympic spirit of achievement made the stadium a reality.

The structure's design has a powerful influence on the way people feel when they experience it.

Big Ideas

The Beijing National Stadium is a defining piece of architecture for 21st-century China. Its oval shape, open roof, translucent membrane-covered walls, and twig-like steel girders give the National Stadium the look of a bird's nest. The original concept for the building did not, however, begin with a nest. Instead, the design was created by studying Chinese ceramics and the patterns that appear when their glaze cracks.

When planning their version of the stadium, the designers wanted to create a vessel, or bowl-like, structure. They also wanted a building that had a porous, or open, feel to it. This was different from traditional Chinese architecture, which tended to be balanced, rectangular, and closed. The openness of the stadium was meant to demonstrate China's modern ideals. The designers also hoped to get people excited about not only the Olympics, but China as well.

The use of steel as a main construction material also had symbolic meaning. China considers itself to be a very powerful country. The steel represented the country's power and strength.

Web Link:
To read more about the ideas behind the National Stadium, go to www.designbuild-network.com/projects/national_stadium

1) The outer supporting framework is made of 24 steel columns, each weighing 1,000 tons (907 tonnes). 2) The structure of the National Stadium is composed of two independent elements, one of steel legs and one of a concrete bowl, standing 50 feet (15.2 meters) apart from each other. 3) As the entrance to the stadium is slightly raised, visitors are treated to a panoramic view of the entire Olympic complex.

Profile:
The "Bird's Nest" Creators

Jacques Herzog

After fierce competition, the winning bid for the design of the National Stadium was finally announced in 2003. The winner was the "Bird's Nest" design proposed by two important Swiss architects, Jacques Herzog and Pierre de Meuron. These two architects are famous for innovative construction using new materials and techniques, including exterior "skins" on buildings. Herzog and de Meuron were both awarded the Pritzker Architecture Prize in 2001. This prize is the highest honor in the field of architecture. They are known for their originality and always "re-inventing" themselves.

Both Herzog and de Meuron were born in Basel, Switzerland, in 1950. They attended the same schools, had similar careers, and in 1978, they formed an architectural firm together. Their firm, called Herzog & de Meuron, has worked on projects all around the world, including the U.S.A., England, France, Germany, Italy, Spain, Japan, China, and Switzerland. These two architects have built all kinds of imaginative buildings together, from factories, offices, and schools, to libraries, museums, and sports complexes.

THE WORK OF HERZOG AND DE MEURON

Signal Box, Basel, Switzerland (1997)
A railway utility building, the Signal Box's exterior is wrapped with 8-inch (20-centimeter) wide copper strips. These strips are twisted at certain places to allow daylight to flood into the interior.

Ricola Distribution Center in Mulhouse-Brunstatt, France (1995)
The building where Ricola cough candies are stored stands out for its unique design. It has translucent walls printed with a plant pattern that becomes less visible as night falls. These walls provide the work areas with a pleasant filtered light.

Dominus Winery in Napa Valley, California (1998)
This winery features a unique wall of stones encased in wire mesh. No **mortar** is used to hold the stones together, giving the wall a very loose, yet imposing, appearance.

It takes a team of talented professionals to develop an iconic structure like the "Bird's Nest." Helping Herzog and de Meuron were Ove Arup and Partners and China Architecture Design and Research Group. These organizations played key roles in the design bid.

Arup, an engineering firm, provided engineering services as well as **acoustics**, fire strategy, sports lighting, and sports architecture for this project. Arup has worked on more than 500 projects in China and is well known for its work on the Sydney Opera House in Australia.

Design advice from the China Design and Architecture Institute provided valuable advice about the design of the structure. The artistic consultant for the design was a Chinese artist named Ai Weiwei.

Ai Weiwei taught Herzog and de Meuron about Chinese design characteristics, which they then included in the architectural design of the "Bird's Nest."

Prada Store in Tokyo, Japan (2003)
This stylish shop is a six-story crystal in Tokyo's fashion district. Its signature diamond-shaped glass panes look like bubbles. The many windows reversed the typical Japanese emphasis on looking inward by giving importance to the view outside.

Tate Modern in London, England (2000)
Herzog & de Meuron converted an old power plant, the Bankside power plant on the Thames River, into an art gallery for modern art. A unique twisting tower is its most noticeable exterior feature. Tate Modern is one of their most highly praised projects.

The Science Behind the Building

The construction of the National Stadium is the result of combining advanced technologies with common building materials. Many scientific studies were associated with this structure's construction. These studies helped to resolve problems encountered during construction.

Withstanding Weight

When building any structure, architects and engineers must consider the structure's load. Loads are forces that act on structures, such as the forces of weight, wind, temperature, or vibration. The weight of a structure itself is called a "dead load." The "live load" includes the weight of people and objects in the building. The weights of both loads, along with the effects of wind, temperature, and vibration, must be calculated before building to ensure that the structure will hold its own weight and the weight of everything inside it.

The National Stadium, made of concrete and steel, is a very heavy structure. The structure itself weighs 45,000 tons (40,824 metric tons). This weight is increased when the stadium is filled with spectators and athletes.

Each of the main structure's steel elements support each other as they interlock, like twigs in a bird's nest. This grid formation is unique in appearance and very strong.

The building needed a solid foundation to support the weight of a full stadium. The structure was built on a **plinth** to help support the "Bird's Nest's" heavy load.

Withstanding Earthquakes

As Beijing is in an earthquake zone, the National Stadium had to be built to withstand Earth's movement in order to protect both people and the structure. Structures should not be too rigid in an earthquake zone. The shockwaves of an earthquake can damage or destroy a building if it is not flexible enough to absorb them. Structural cracks were common in buildings built before earthquake science was used in building design.

The "Bird's Nest" can withstand an earthquake up to a magnitude of eight on the **Richter Scale**. This was accomplished by building the structure in two separate parts, one for the steel structure, and one for the concrete bowl. Also, the spectator stands in the concrete bowl were built as eight zones, like eight separate buildings, each with its own stability system. Should one zone move due to an earthquake, it will not affect the other zones.

Web Link:
For more information about calculating building loads, visit www.pbs.org/wgbh/buildingbig/lab/loads.html

Science and Technology

To bring the design of the National Stadium to life, engineers and construction workers had to use a range of equipment and technology. Some of the processes and tools were modern, while others relied on the science of simple machines. Many cranes were used to do the heavy lifting and help properly position the heavy steel and concrete elements of the structure. Several methods were used to put the pieces together.

Cranes are often used to build high-rise structures.

Pulleys

A pulley is a wheel with a grooved rim through which a belt or chain is guided. Pulleys help raise and lower heavy loads by changing the direction of a pulling force. Cranes are machines that lift and move heavy construction materials and equipment into place. They use pulleys to operate. These machines were very important in the construction of the "Bird's Nest." Cranes were used to lift and place the many steel beams and columns into their proper position.

Precast Concrete

Concrete can set to any shape or form, but it needs to harden inside a container called a cast. When concrete hardens in a cast, it takes on the shape and size of the cast. Sometimes, concrete is poured into its casts on the construction site. In some cases, however, it is poured into its cast at a different location and then shipped to the job site. When this is done, the concrete is called precast. For the National Stadium, the designers chose to use precast concrete for the stadium's middle and upper levels.

Concrete is poured into casts to create different shapes and sizes.

By setting the concrete into its desired shapes and sizes before construction began, they did not have to wait for it to harden. This saved time on the construction site and made the installation process run more smoothly.

Welding

With its "legs" of steel and complicated steel skeleton, welding was a very important element of construction for the "Bird's Nest." Welding uses heat to cut metal or join it together. It is used in many forms of construction, including bridge and building construction, as well as car-making.

There are several different welding processes. Which is used depends on the type of metal, its size and shape, and how strong the finished product needs to be. Electric arc welding, which creates heat as an electric current, is often used to weld thin pieces of metal. Gas welding, which produces more heat, is best used when fusing thick pieces together.

Welders worked during hot summer weather, heating steel to 302 degrees Fahrenheit (150 degrees Celsius), in order to bond pieces together.

Welding must take place as a continuous process to ensure a strong bond between two pieces of steel. Strong bonds allow the two pieces of steel to work together in bearing the weight of a structure. If the process is stopped, the joint will be weakened, possibly making it unsafe.

Quick Bites

- One welding project on the "Bird's Nest" took 17 hours to complete. Different workers had to take turns on this job to avoid exhaustion. Some welds had to be made in tight places, sometimes with workers hanging upside down to reach the right spot.
- Carved into each joint of the stadium is the name of the welder in charge of that joint. Although they cannot be seen now, the names of these welders will go down in history.

Computer-Aided Design

Architects are trained professionals who work with clients to design structures. Before anything is built, they make detailed drawings or models. These plans are important tools that help people visualize what the structure will look like. A blueprint is a detailed diagram that shows where all the parts of the structure will be placed. Walls, doors, windows, plumbing, electrical wiring, and other details are mapped out on the blueprint. Blueprints act as a guide for engineers and builders during construction.

For centuries, architects and builders worked without the aid of computers. Sketches and blueprints were drawn by hand. Highly skilled drafters would draw very technical designs. Today, this process is done using computers and sophisticated software programs. Architects use CAD, or computer-aided design, throughout the design process. Early CAD systems used computers to draft building plans. Today's computer programs can do much more. They can build three-dimensional models and computer simulations of how a building will look. They can also calculate the effects of different physical forces on the structure. Using CAD, today's architects can build more complex structures at lower cost and in less time.

Computer-aided design programs have been used since the 1960s.

Eye on Design

Seating Software

The inner concrete seating bowl houses the spectator stands and athletic fields.

The National Stadium was designed with spectators in mind. The 91,000 seats inside the building had to be positioned in a way that would ensure all spectators had a good view. However, it also created many design challenges.

For example, moving the first row of seats just a few inches could make a huge difference in the building's dimensions. In order to deal with these challenges, computer software was developed to help design the "Bird's Nest." This **parametric** design program helped the designers work out the **geometry** of the stadium.

Designers used the software to develop different seating scenarios. In doing this, they could see how putting seats in certain positions and at certain angles affected a viewer's ability to see the events on the ground. The program showed them how to place the seats in the stadium and how to build the stadium's bowl so that all spectators felt that they had good seats. Using this program, the farthest seat is only 460 feet (140 m) from center field.

MEASURING THE BEIJING NATIONAL STADIUM

Location

The National Stadium is located at the south end of Olympic Green, a large public area dedicated to Olympic venues in Beijing, China's capital city.

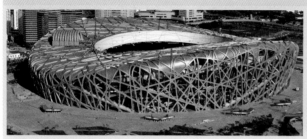

Area and Volume

The **gross** floor area of the National Stadium is 64 acres (258,000 square meters).

The stadium measures 965 feet (294 m) from east to west and 1,093 feet (333 m) from north to south.

The structure has a **volume** of 3,923,851 cubic yards (3 million cubic meters).

Height

- At almost 20 stories high, the National Stadium's maximum height is 226 feet (69 m).

Weight

The steel components of this structure weigh a colossal 42,000 tons (38,102 metric tons). The total weight of the structure without spectators is 45,000 tons (40,824 metric tons).

Other Interesting Facts

- More than 7,000 cement workers helped to build the National Stadium.
- Red, a traditional Chinese color, is found in many places in the "Bird's Nest." A red glow from the structure's outer membrane lights up the night sky. Service counters are painted red, red-colored glass is used as an accent, and many of the seats are red.

Environmental Viewpoint

One of Beijing's goals for the Olympics was to host a "green" event. City officials wanted the structures created for the games to have minimal impact on the environment. Building "green" facilities was one way the city planned to accomplish this goal. As a result, the "Bird's Nest" was designed for low environmental impact and environmental **sustainability**.

The stadium's open roof contributes much to sustainability. If the building had a closed roof, it would need to rely on artificial lighting and **ventilation** systems, both of which can consume a great deal of energy. The open roof allows for natural ventilation using normal airflow. Natural light also enters the building through the open roof as well as through the translucent membrane that is wrapped around the building. This greatly reduces the need for large electrical systems.

A 24-hour rainwater collection system conserves water and saves energy, too. Rainwater that comes in through the open roof is collected in drainage systems, where it is filtered and cleaned. Following this process, the water is used in the stadium's washrooms and for **irrigation** purposes.

When designing the building, the planners placed special pipes under the stadium's playing surface. These pipes use advanced technology to gather heat from the soil in the winter and cold from the soil in the summer. These pipes help the stadium control its temperature naturally.

The eco-friendly stadium includes several "green" technologies.

BEIJING'S "GREEN" OLYMPICS

Beijing, a city of approximately 14 million people, overcame several environmental challenges associated with hosting the 2008 Summer Olympics.

Air pollution due to industry, coal-burning, and traffic was a major health concern for the Olympic athletes. Beijing took its air pollution problem seriously and spent more than $15 billion on anti-pollution measures.

Anti-pollution measures included moving factories, adding subway lines to reduce traffic congestion, and converting coal-heated homes to electric heat. Olympics and Paralympics authorities asked some factories to close and forced many heavy polluters to reduce their **emissions** by 30 percent. Private vehicles, including taxis, were ordered to stay off the roads every other day to reduce emissions, too.

Trees help scrub the air of pollutants. More than 2,700 trees were planted around the "Bird's Nest," providing an attractive landscape as well as a practical anti-pollution measure.

Construction Careers

It takes all kinds of talent to build an iconic structure. Thousands of people, including architects, engineers, concrete workers, steelworkers, welders, plumbers, electricians, crane operators, general laborers, and others, all played an important role in the construction of Beijing's landmark structure, the National Stadium.

Welders

Welders join and separate metals in beams, girders, vessels, piping, tools, machines, equipment, and other metal parts. Welding can be risky as it involves torches and hot metals. The process itself creates sparks and fumes. Welders are expected to make their own patterns for a project or be able to follow directions in layouts and blueprints. Welders need to be good at working with their hands, and have good vision, the ability to concentrate on detailed work, and patience. Work in this profession is performed both indoors and outdoors, sometimes at remote job sites. Companies involved in construction, vessel or structural steel assembly, pipelines, steel fabrication and heavy equipment repair hire welders.

Concrete Finisher

Construction workers that specialize in concrete are called concrete finishers. They work both indoors and out, depending on the task. Concrete finishers pour wet concrete into casts and spread it to a desired thickness. They level and smooth the surface and edges of concrete. To give the concrete different effects, they apply various finishes to the surface, including broomed, smooth, and patterned effects. Concrete finishers also repair, waterproof, and restore concrete surfaces. This physical work involves bending, stooping, kneeling, and lifting heavy bags of cement. Concrete finishers must know how to age or cure concrete perfectly in order for this construction material to have maximum strength.

Structural Engineer

Structural engineering is a specialty of civil engineering. Civil engineering includes the planning, design, construction, maintenance, and removal of structures, from buildings to oil rigs. Structural engineers often work with architects, other engineers, and construction contractors. Structural engineers help design load-bearing structures, such as roofs, bridges, towers, and buildings. They carry out inspections at different stages of the building process to make sure the structure can withstand different forces, such as wind, rain, and vibration. Structural engineers make sure structures are built safe, strong, and stable.

Web Link:
To find out more about jobs in construction, visit
http://careers.nccer.org

Notable Structures

China is home to many unique structures, ranging from ancient to modern in age. Most of these structures were built for a definite purpose at a specific time. Even though their purpose may no longer exist, many of these structures have captured the attention of the world.

Great Wall of China

Built: 221 BC to 1644 AD

Location: Along a portion of China's inland boundary

Design: Built by different emperors over time

Description: The Great Wall of China was built to protect China from Mongolian invaders. This structure is about 1,500 miles (2,414 km) long and runs from Kansu in the west to the Yellow Sea in the east. The wall is so large it can be seen from outer space.

The Forbidden City

Built: 1407 to 1420 AD

Location: Beijing, China

Design: Ming Dynasty

Description: The Forbidden City was the royal palace of China's rulers for five centuries. The complex contains about 9,000 rooms in its five halls, 17 palaces, and other buildings. A deep moat and a tall wall surround the Forbidden City. Housing many rare treasures, it was named a **UNESCO World Cultural Heritage Site** in 1987.

Innovation in design and the effective use of materials have made certain structures withstand the tests of both time and imagination.

Jin Mao Tower

Built: 1999

Location: Shanghai, China

Design: Skidmore, Owings, and Merrill

Description: The Jin Mao Tower is one of the tallest structures in the world. It is a skyscraper that contains both offices and a hotel. The tower's design borrows heavily from traditional Chinese architecture. Its shape resembles that of a pagoda, or Chinese temple.

National Aquatics Center

Built: 2008

Location: Beijing, China

Design: PTW Architects of Australia

Description: The shiny, square, blue-colored building is also known as the "Water Cube." It was built to host swimming events for the 2008 Summer Olympics in Beijing. The Water Cube is completely wrapped in a membrane covering. Its 3,065 exterior air cushions make the building look like it is made out of water bubbles.

Structural Icons Around the World

Structures that inspire the human imagination have been built all around the world. Some were built by ancient civilizations. Others were built in modern times.

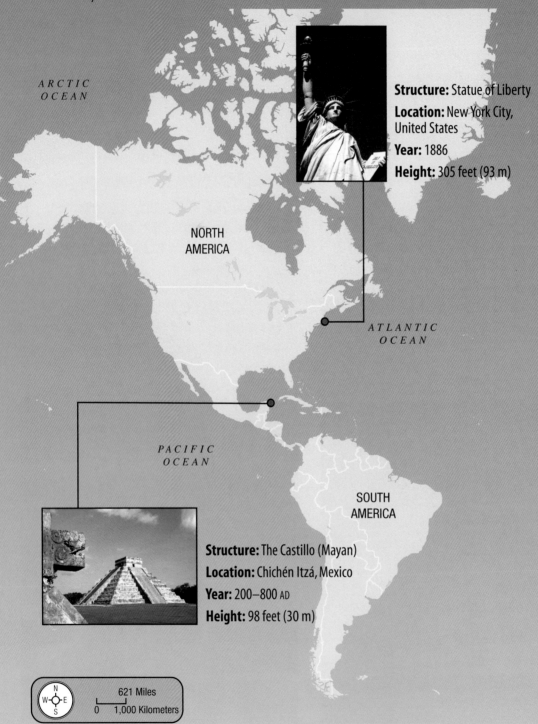

Structure: Statue of Liberty

Location: New York City, United States

Year: 1886

Height: 305 feet (93 m)

ARCTIC OCEAN

NORTH AMERICA

ATLANTIC OCEAN

PACIFIC OCEAN

SOUTH AMERICA

Structure: The Castillo (Mayan)

Location: Chichén Itzá, Mexico

Year: 200–800 AD

Height: 98 feet (30 m)

N
W—E
S

621 Miles

0   1,000 Kilometers

Many magnificent structures have become symbols of nations. This map shows some of the structures that have come to symbolize the country in which they reside.

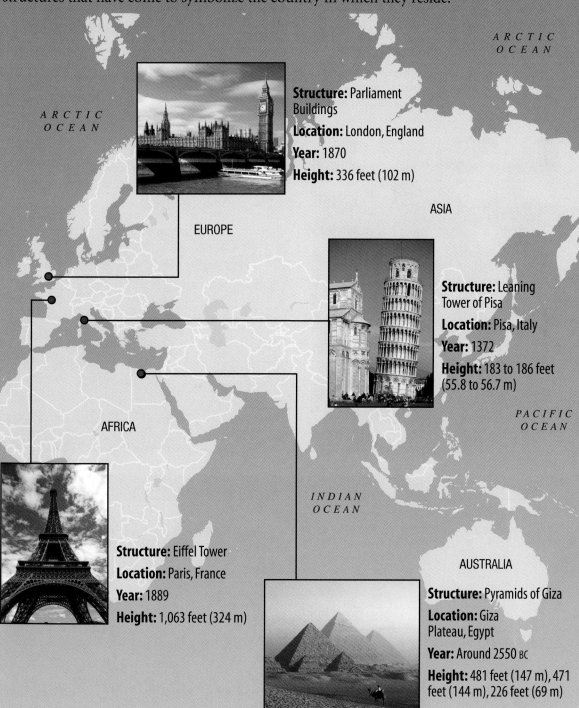

ARCTIC OCEAN

ARCTIC OCEAN

Structure: Parliament Buildings

Location: London, England

Year: 1870

Height: 336 feet (102 m)

ASIA

EUROPE

Structure: Leaning Tower of Pisa

Location: Pisa, Italy

Year: 1372

Height: 183 to 186 feet (55.8 to 56.7 m)

AFRICA

PACIFIC OCEAN

INDIAN OCEAN

Structure: Eiffel Tower

Location: Paris, France

Year: 1889

Height: 1,063 feet (324 m)

AUSTRALIA

Structure: Pyramids of Giza

Location: Giza Plateau, Egypt

Year: Around 2550 BC

Height: 481 feet (147 m), 471 feet (144 m), 226 feet (69 m)

Quiz

Q What was the reason for building the National Stadium?

A The National Stadium was built to serve as the main venue for the 2008 Summer Olympics. The opening and closing ceremonies were held at the National Stadium. Track and field events as well as soccer and athletics were held there, too.

Q Where is the National Stadium located?

A The National Stadium is located in Beijing, China.

Q How heavy is the Beijing National Stadium?

A The massive National Stadium weighs about 45,000 tons (40,824 metric tons) without spectators in it.

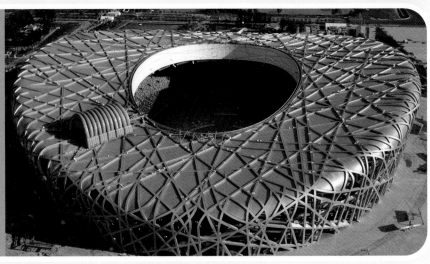

Q Why is the National Stadium nicknamed the "Bird's Nest"?

A The National Stadium is called the "Bird's Nest" because of its look and shape. Exterior steel components crisscross to look like the twigs of a bird's nest.

The Nest Test

Birds build nests using just their beaks. Often made of twigs, grass, and mud, these delicate looking structures are strong enough to bear the weight of eggs and adult birds. These small miracles of construction sometimes last many years and raise several generations of birds. Test your architectural skills by building a bird's nest of your own.

Materials

- Twigs
- Mud (dirt and water)
- Grass
- Straw
- Small leaves (if available)
- Bits of fluff (scraps of material or yarn, facial tissue, etc.)
- Hard-boiled eggs
- 3 rulers or thick sticks about 12 inches (30 cm) long
- Tape

Instructions

1. Use the mud to mold the twigs, leaves, grass, and straw into a nest. The nest should be round or oval in shape, and high enough to have a cup-shaped pit in the center. Line the nest with soft bits of fluff, grass, and small leaves. Let the nest dry.

2. Once your nest is dry, take it outside, and place it in a bush or a tree. Try to find a secure spot for it so it will not fall out or tip over. Be careful not to break any branches as you position your nest.

3. If you do not have a bush or tree, use three long sticks or rulers to make a triangle that can support the nest. Use tape to keep the sticks or rulers in place. Then, position the nest in the triangle.

4. Place the eggs, one at a time, in the nest.

5. Observe how many eggs the nest can hold without breaking or tipping. Gently press down on one side of the nest to mimic a bird landing. Does your structure tip or break?

6. Consider how your structure could be stronger. Does it need a stronger foundation? Would less mud and more twigs make it stronger? Would the eggs be more secure in a deeper or wider cup?

Further Research

You can find more information on the National Stadium, Beijing Olympics, and Chinese architecture at your local library or on the Internet.

Websites

For more information on the National Stadium, visit the official website of the Beijing 2008 Olympic Games at http://en.beijing2008.cn/venues/nst

To view the National Stadium's construction process, visit http://en.beijing2008.cn/cptvenues/venues/nst/headlines/nstready/s214370212

To see more examples of modern Chinese architecture, visit www.chinese-architecture.info/TEN/TEN-CHINA.htm

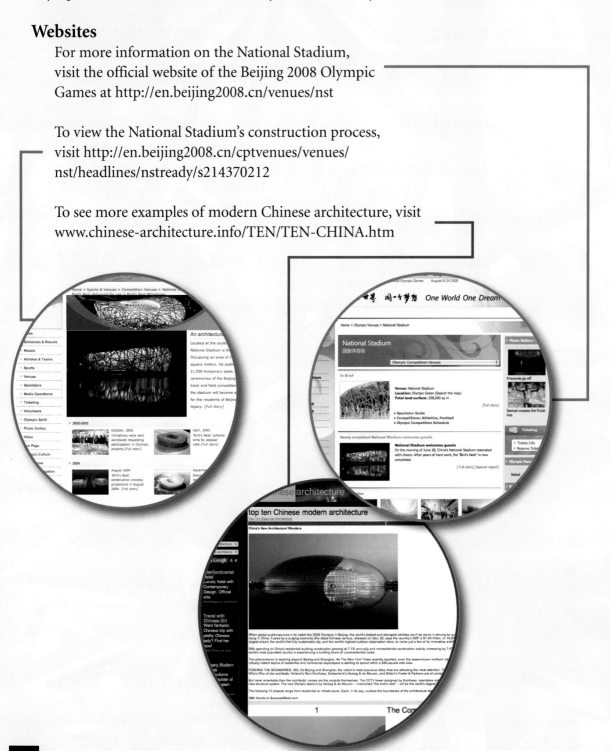

Glossary

acoustics: relating to the sense of hearing

architects: people who design and supervise the construction of buildings

ceramics: the art of producing objects out of clay or porcelain

emissions: substances that are sent into the air

geometry: the branch of mathematics that is concerned with the measurements of lines, curves, and surfaces

girders: large beams

gross: a total amount

groundbreaking ceremonies: events which mark the beginning of construction

iconic: something that is symbolic

irrigation: a water supply system

latticework: a framework of metal or wood that forms a decorative pattern

membrane: a thin, soft, flexible layer or sheet

mortar: a mixture of sand, cement, and water that is used to bond materials together

parametric: relating to a constant or limiting factor

plinth: a base upon which statues and structures are placed

retractable: having the ability to draw in

Richter scale: a scale that tells how serious an earthquake is

sustainability: being able to use a resource so that it is not depleted or permanently damaged

UNESCO World Cultural Heritage Site: a site designated by the United Nations to be of great cultural worth to the world and in need of protection

ventilation: a system that supplies fresh air

volume: the amount of space enclosed within an object

Index

Beijing, China 5, 6, 10, 13, 19, 20, 21, 22, 24, 25, 28, 30

China Design and Architecture Institute 11
concrete 7, 8, 12, 13, 14, 15, 22, 23

de Meuron, Pierre 10, 11

earthquakes 13
environment 20, 21

Forbidden City 24

Great Wall of China 24

Herzog, Jacques 10, 11

Jin Mao Tower 25

load 12, 13, 23

National Aquatics Center 25

Olympic Games 5, 6, 7, 10, 20, 21, 25, 28, 30
Ove Arup and Partners 11

pulley 14

roof 5, 6, 7, 8, 20, 23

seats 7, 17, 19
steel 5, 6, 7, 8, 12, 13, 14, 15, 19, 22, 28

ventilation 20

water 20, 25, 29
Weiwei, Ai 11
welding 7, 15, 22

JAN   2010

CLIFTON PARK-HALFMOON PUBLIC LIBRARY, NY

0 00 06 0349721 5